# KiD SCiENCE

## BACKYARD SCiENCE EXPERiMENTS

Q. L. Pearce

LOWELL HOUSE JUVENILE

LOS ANGELES

NTC/Contemporary Publishing Group

*With love to Kaitlyn Makenzie Pearce,*
*my inspiration*
*—Q. P.*

Published by Lowell House
A division of NTC/Contemporary Publishing Group, Inc.
4255 West Touhy Avenue, Lincolnwood (Chicago), Illinois 60646-1975 U.S.A.

Lowell House books can be purchased at special discounts when ordered in bulk for premiums and special sales. Contact Department CS at the following address:

NTC/Contemporary Publishing Group
4255 West Touhy Avenue
Lincolnwood, IL 60646-1975
1-800-323-4900

ISBN: 0-7373-9863-9
Library of Congress Catalog Card Number: 99-74664

Roxbury Park is a division of NTC/Contemporary Publishing Group, Inc.

Managing Director and Publisher: Jack Artenstein
Editor in Chief, Roxbury Park Books: Michael Artenstein
Director of Publishing Services: Rena Copperman
Editorial Assistant: Nicole Monastirsky
Freelance Editor: Sara Gooch
Interior Artist: Sophie Sheppard
Interior Designer: Carolyn Wendt

Printed and Bound in Mexico
00 01 RDD 10 9 8 7 6 5 4 3 2

# CONTENTS

**W**hat is soil made of? Do plants breathe? What do snails eat? The answers to these questions and more are as near as your own backyard. With a few simple materials, you can set up your own weather station, start a spider web collection, or count the stars in the night sky.

Here are some basic safety tips:

- Before you begin, read the directions completely.

- Wear old clothing or an apron.

- Never put an unknown material into your mouth or near your eyes.

- Ask permission before digging any holes.

- Be careful not to harm living things.

- Clean your work area when you are finished.

- Wash your hands when you are finished.

Most of the materials you'll need for these experiments are probably already in your home. Check with an adult before you use any household supplies. You may need an adult helper for some of the experiments in this book.

Are you ready for some fun? Then let's go outside and get started.

# STAY COOL

*Desert animals have different methods of staying cool. Some are active at night when the air temperature is cooler than in the daytime. Some animals spend the day in an underground burrow. This experiment will show why that strategy works.*

**Setup time:** 20 minutes • **Observation time:** 10 minutes

## MATERIALS

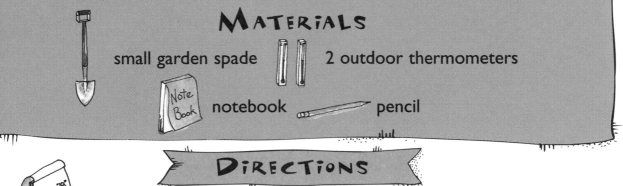

small garden spade          2 outdoor thermometers

notebook          pencil

## DIRECTIONS

**1.** In a shady spot, check the temperature of both thermometers to be sure that they match. Record the temperature in your notebook.

**2.** In a sunny spot, where it's okay to dig, dig a hole 6″ (15 cm) deep in the soil large enough to hold one thermometer.

**3.** Bury the first thermometer in the hole, covering it lightly with dirt. Lay the other thermometer on the top of the soil facing the sun.

**4.** After 10 minutes, record the temperature of the thermometer in the sun. Quickly dig up the buried thermometer and record the temperature.

10 minutes

## ACTION, REACTION, RESULTS

The earth is heated by the rays of the sun. The buried thermometer is shielded from the sun's direct rays by a layer of soil. It does not get as hot as the other thermometer. Desert animals can also find shelter from the sun by burrowing under the soil where it is cooler.

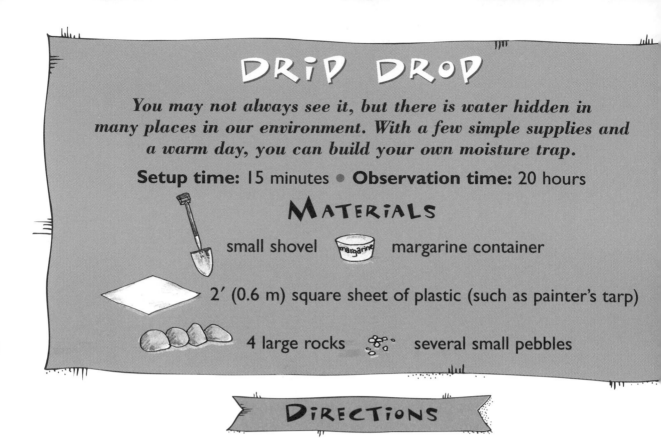

# DRIP DROP

*You may not always see it, but there is water hidden in many places in our environment. With a few simple supplies and a warm day, you can build your own moisture trap.*

**Setup time:** 15 minutes ● **Observation time:** 20 hours

## MATERIALS

small shovel    margarine container

2′ (0.6 m) square sheet of plastic (such as painter's tarp)

4 large rocks    several small pebbles

## DIRECTIONS

1. Start this experiment on a warm, sunny day. Find a spot in your yard where it is okay to dig. Dig a cone-shaped hole about 18″ (45 cm) across at the top, 6″ (15 cm) across at the bottom, and 1′ (30 cm) deep.

2. Place an open, empty margarine container at the bottom of the hole.

3. Spread the plastic sheet out flat over the hole and secure it at each corner with a rock.

**4.** Pile the pebbles in the center of the plastic so that the plastic sags toward the margarine container.

**5.** Leave everything in place overnight. Check the margarine container for moisture the following morning.

## ACTION, REACTION, RESULTS

Soil, even desert soil, contains some water. The air contains water, too. Water from lakes, rivers, and other sources evaporates into the air and becomes water vapor. In your experiment, the warmth of the sun causes water in the soil to evaporate. Warm air holds more water vapor than cold air. As the air cools at night, condensation forms on the plastic. Drops of water roll down the plastic and drip into the container at the bottom of the hole.

**WORD FILE**

**Condensation:** Liquid formed by cooling a vapor.

**Evaporate:** To change liquid into a vapor using heat or moving air.

Building a moisture trap can be a lifesaver for someone lost in a desert when even a small drink of water can make a difference.

# HERE COMES THE SUN

*You can tell time without a watch by building this solar timepiece in your backyard.*

**Setup time:** 8 hours • **Observation time:** ongoing on sunny days

## MATERIALS

stiff cardboard · ruler · pencil · scissors · lid to a cardboard shoe box at least 6" (15 cm) wide · protractor 6" (15 cm) high · compass · watch

## DIRECTIONS

1. Prepare your sundial early in the morning or the night before you intend to mark it. Draw a triangle on the stiff cardboard. It must have two 6" (15 cm) sides at a right angle to each other. The third side will be about 8" (20 cm) long. At the base of the triangle, draw a ½" (1.5 cm) wide strip, as shown.

2. Cut out the triangle and strip in one piece to form a triangle with a ½" (1.5 cm) tab at the base.

3. Use the protractor to draw a semicircle on the top of the shoe box lid, as shown. Draw a line across the width of the lid at the center. Cut a slit along the line. Slip the tab of the triangle into the slit so that the triangle stands up straight and at a right angle to the lid.

**4.** With the triangle pointing north and south, place the lid in a location that's sunny all day.

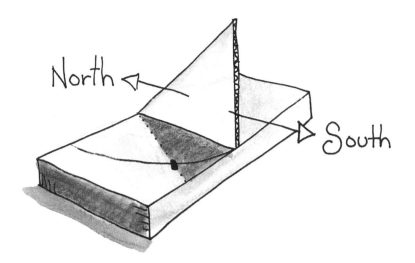

**5.** Begin early in the morning. On the hour, make a line on the lid where the shadow falls and write the hour at that mark. Repeat the process every hour marking the hours until sundown.

## ACTION, REACTION, RESULTS

The triangle on your sundial is called a gnomon. The angle of the shadow that it casts depends on the position of the sun. The sun appears to move across the sky from east to west in a path called the ecliptic. As it completes its daily journey, the angle on the sundial changes hour to hour, but the pattern is the same each day. Once you have marked your sundial, you will be able to use it to tell the time whenever the sun is up.

**WORD FILE**

**Angle:** The area between two lines that meet. An angle is measured in degrees.

**Ecliptic:** The sun's apparent path through the sky relative to the stars.

**Gnomon:** The raised portion of a sundial that casts a shadow.

The earliest known sundial is from Egypt, and it is three thousand years old!

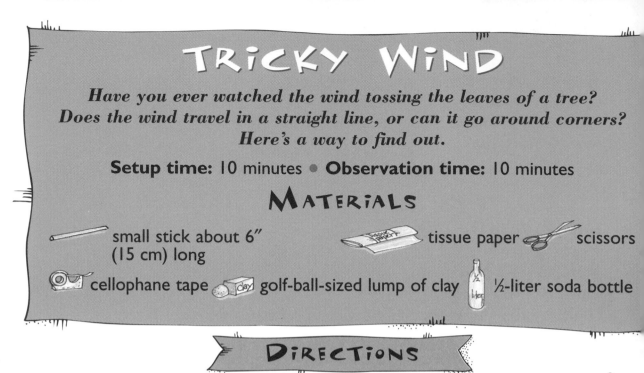

# TRICKY WIND

*Have you ever watched the wind tossing the leaves of a tree?*
*Does the wind travel in a straight line, or can it go around corners?*
*Here's a way to find out.*

**Setup time:** 10 minutes ● **Observation time:** 10 minutes

## MATERIALS

small stick about 6" (15 cm) long • tissue paper • scissors

cellophane tape • golf-ball-sized lump of clay • ½-liter soda bottle

## DIRECTIONS

**1.** Cut a strip of tissue paper about 2" (5 cm) long and about 1" (2.5 cm) wide. Make a series of small 1" (2.5 cm) long slits at one end. Tape the uncut end around one end of the stick.

**2.** On a flat surface, push the other end of the stick into the clay so that it stands up straight. Place the bottle next to the stick, leaving about ½" (1.5 cm) of space between them.

**3.** Position yourself so you are at eye level with the bottle on the opposite side from the stick. With the bottle between you and the stick, blow toward the top of the stick. Does the tissue paper flutter?

## ACTION, REACTION, RESULTS

Air flows toward areas of low pressure. The molecules of air flowing past a curved surface speed up, lowering the pressure at the surface and causing the air flow to curve also. The stream of air you blow toward the bottle splits and flows around the bottle, then joins on the other side and continues to flow in a straight line. Even though it is behind the bottle, the tissue paper will blow in the wind.

**10**

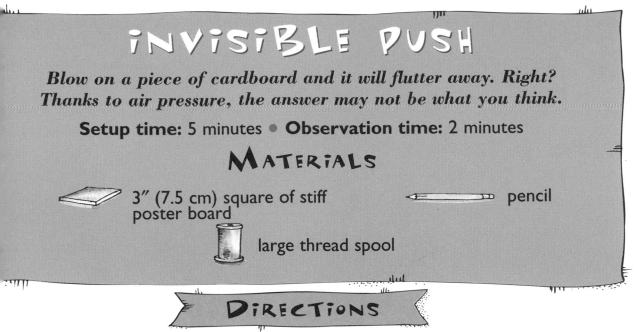

# INVISIBLE PUSH

*Blow on a piece of cardboard and it will flutter away. Right?*
*Thanks to air pressure, the answer may not be what you think.*

**Setup time:** 5 minutes • **Observation time:** 2 minutes

## MATERIALS

3" (7.5 cm) square of stiff poster board

pencil

large thread spool

## DIRECTIONS

**1.** Draw a straight line from one corner to the diagonal corner on the cardboard square. Draw another diagonal line from corner to corner, creating an **X**.

**2.** Where the two lines cross is the center of the square. Hold the thread spool in your right hand and the square in your left. Place the thread spool on the square so that the hole in the spool lines up with the center of the **X**. Hold the square in place with the flat of your hand.

**3.** Blow down through the hole in the spool and let go with your left hand. Does the cardboard just blow away?

## ACTION, REACTION, RESULTS

The card tends to stay in place because the moving air creates an area of low pressure. The pressure of the air pushing up on the card is greater than the pressure pushing down on it. The card is held up by air pressure pushing against it.

# WILD WEBS

*Spiders are among the world's smallest predators, and they have a unique way of catching their prey. They build a trap . . . a web. Here's a way to gather, study, and display a unique collection of spider webs.*

**Setup time:** 20 minutes • **Observation time:** as desired

## MATERIALS

can of clear spray lacquer (available in hardware stores)

8″ (20 cm) square sheet of stiff black paper

## DIRECTIONS

1. Look around your yard or a nearby park for a spider web. Touch the center of the web lightly with a leaf to be sure that the weaver is no longer around. If the spider is on or near the web, don't disturb the spider or the web. Find a web with no spider.

2. Spray the web with lacquer several times, allowing it to dry between applications.

**3.** Spray the web once again. While the web is still wet, hold the black paper up against it and lift the web onto the paper. Gently pull away any support strands.

**4.** Spray the web and paper with one more layer of lacquer and allow it to dry.

**5.** Follow the same procedure with other webs. Look for different sizes and shapes.

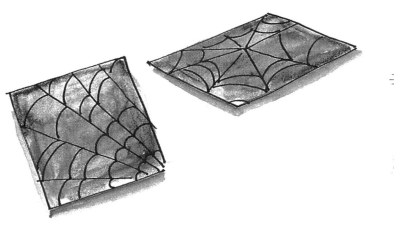

**WORD FILE**

**Predator:** An animal that kills and eats other animals.

**Prey:** An animal used by a predator as food.

Many spiders weave a new web every day. Some eat the old web. To find out the habits of the creature that spun the web you have collected, check in a field guide to spiders.

# FREE FRESH AIR

*The next time you take a deep breath, thank a plant.*
*Much of the oxygen in the air we breath is provided by plants*
*as a by-product of their food-making process.*

**Setup time:** 5 minutes ● **Observation time:** I hour

## MATERIALS

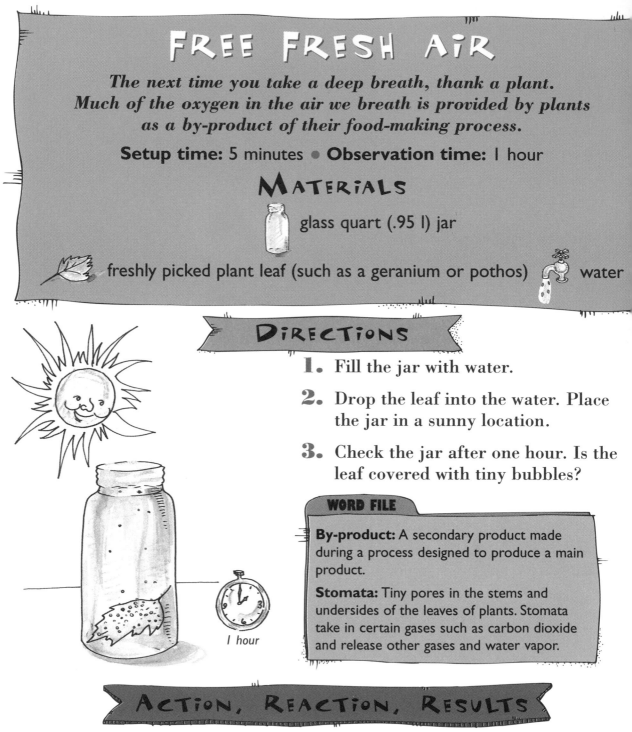

glass quart (.95 l) jar

freshly picked plant leaf (such as a geranium or pothos)      water

## DIRECTIONS

**1.** Fill the jar with water.

**2.** Drop the leaf into the water. Place the jar in a sunny location.

**3.** Check the jar after one hour. Is the leaf covered with tiny bubbles?

### WORD FILE

**By-product:** A secondary product made during a process designed to produce a main product.

**Stomata:** Tiny pores in the stems and undersides of the leaves of plants. Stomata take in certain gases such as carbon dioxide and release other gases and water vapor.

I hour

## ACTION, REACTION, RESULTS

Plants use sunlight, air, and water to make their own food. The process is called photosynthesis. One of the by-products of photosynthesis is oxygen, which is released into the air through the stomata on a plant's leaves. The bubbles you see in this experiment are bubbles of oxygen.

**14**

# THE BETTER TO SEE YOU WITH

*If you want to get a closer look at some small object in nature, a drop of water can help.*

**Setup time:** 5 minutes ● **Observation time:** 5 minutes

## MATERIALS

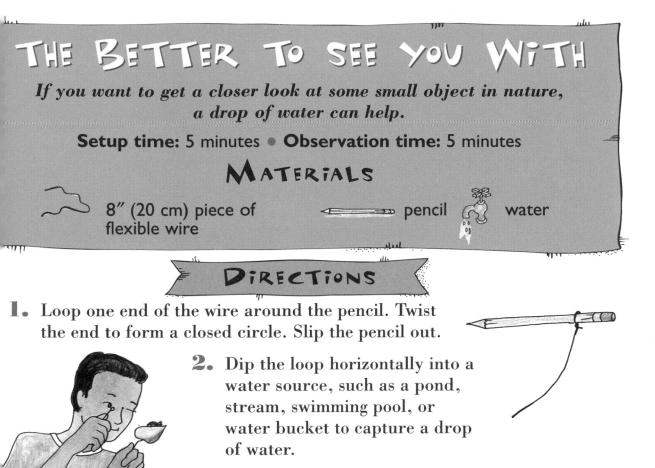

8" (20 cm) piece of flexible wire

pencil

water

## DIRECTIONS

**1.** Loop one end of the wire around the pencil. Twist the end to form a closed circle. Slip the pencil out.

**2.** Dip the loop horizontally into a water source, such as a pond, stream, swimming pool, or water bucket to capture a drop of water.

**3.** Observe any small object through the water drop. Does it appear slightly larger?

## ACTION, REACTION, RESULTS

The water drop becomes a simple lens. Light rays passing through the outwardly curved, or convex, water drop are brought to a focus at one point, which causes objects viewed through the drop to appear larger.

The lens of the eye is convex. Sometimes it may be slightly misshapen, making it hard to see properly either up close or at a distance. The corrective lenses in eyeglasses make up for the problem.

**WORD FILE**

**Convex:** Outwardly curved. The opposite is concave, or inwardly curved.

**Lens:** A piece of curved, transparent material, usually glass or plastic.

# KEEPING TRACK

*Many of the Earth's creatures have become extinct, but some have left behind traces in the form of fossils. You can get an idea of how fossils form by making some of your own.*

**Setup time:** 15 minutes ● **Observation time:** 30 minutes

## MATERIALS

2 margarine containers    clay    cooking spray

small seashell    plaster of paris    water

## DIRECTIONS

**1.** Flatten a ½″ (1.5 cm) deep layer of clay in the bottom of a margarine container. Spray the layer with cooking spray.

**2.** Press the seashell into the clay, then remove it to leave a deep impression.

If you find an interesting animal track in the dirt, you can preserve it by using plaster of paris. Make a circle of a long, thin strip of cardboard held in place with a paper clip or tape. Push the circle into the soil around the track, then pour the plaster of paris inside the circle. Lift the hardened plaster when it dries.

**3.** In another margarine container, mix ½ cup of plaster of paris according to package directions. Pour the mixture over the clay, covering it completely. Allow the plaster to dry for about 30 minutes.

30 minutes

**4.** Pop the finished piece out of the container. Carefully peel off the clay and observe your homemade fossil.

## ACTION, REACTION, RESULTS

The impression you made is an example of a kind of trace fossil. For example, an animal such as a dinosaur may have walked on the banks of a stream, leaving its footprints behind in the same way that the shell left an impression in the clay. If the footprint simply dried and hardened, it would be preserved as a cast fossil. Another possibility is that the stream may have flooded, filling the prints with mud in the same way that the plaster of paris filled the impression in the clay. Once the mud dried, the result would be a mold fossil.

**WORD FILE**

**Trace fossil:** Fossil evidence left behind by living things. Trace fossils may be footprints, droppings, or impressions of plants or animals.

# WATER LOSS

*Take a walk around your neighborhood and you are likely to see many different kinds of plants with leaves of different shapes and textures. Does the surface and shape of a leaf have an effect on the plant? This demonstration will show one way that it does.*

**Setup time:** 15 minutes ● **Observation time:** 2 hours

## MATERIALS

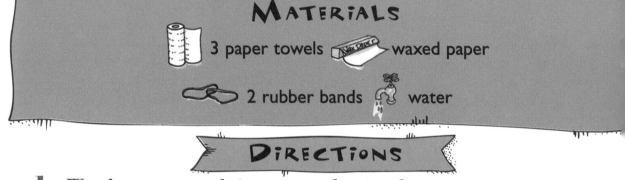

3 paper towels — waxed paper

2 rubber bands — water

## DIRECTIONS

**1.** Wet the paper towels in water and wring them out.

**2.** Spread out the first paper towel on a flat surface in a sunny area.

**3.** Roll the second paper towel into a cylinder shape and place it beside the first.

**4.** Roll the third paper towel into a cylinder shape and cover it completely with waxed paper. Seal the ends of the waxed paper roll with rubber bands. Place it with the other towels.

**5.** After 2 hours spread each of the towels out and check for moisture.

## ACTION, REACTION, RESULTS

The flat paper towel is the driest, the rolled paper towel is damp inside, and the waxed-paper-covered towel is the wettest. The greater the surface area of an object, the faster the moisture in it will evaporate. That is why the flat towel dried out the fastest. The rolled up shape of the second paper towel helped it to retain moisture, while the waxy coating around the third paper towel kept it very damp.

**18**

# THE AIR DOWN UNDER

*When your feet feel good you may feel like you are walking on air.*
*In fact, even though you are firmly on the ground,*
*there is some air beneath your feet.*

**Setup time:** 15 minutes ● **Observation time:** 10 minutes

## MATERIALS

1 cup (240 ml) of water that has been boiled and allowed to cool

glass quart (.95 l) jar

1 cup of dry soil

## DIRECTIONS

**1.** Pour the soil into the clean quart (.95 l) jar.

**2.** Slowly pour the water over the soil, covering it completely.

**3.** Place the jar on a flat surface and observe from the side. Do you see small bubbles rising from the soil through the water?

## ACTION, REACTION, RESULTS

Soil is made up of many different materials, including tiny grains of rock, some finer than others. These grains do not fit together perfectly, so there are spaces in between. Air is trapped in the spaces. When you pour water into the jar, it fills the spaces and forces the air out in the form of bubbles.

# DINNER GUESTS

*Sometimes it seems that snails will eat anything and everything in the garden. With close observation, you can discover what these hungry creatures like best.*

**Setup time:** 30 minutes • **Observation time:** 2 or 3 days

## MATERIALS

empty aquarium or large glass jar — black construction paper

paper towels — aluminum foil — several small rocks

sample foods such as lettuce and other garden leaves

2 or 3 garden snails (found in cool, moist areas)

cheesecloth — string — scissors

## DIRECTIONS

**1.** To prepare a habitat for your snails in an aquarium or large glass jar, first cover the bottom of the area with black construction paper.

**2.** Moisten a paper towel, crumple it, and place it in a corner of the habitat. Put it on a square of aluminum foil so that it doesn't dampen the construction paper. Be sure to keep the paper towel very moist as long as the snails are in the habitat.

**3.** Place small rocks around the edges of the habitat for the snails to crawl on.

**4.** Put a different food source in each corner of the habitat.

**5.** Cover the opening with cheesecloth and tie it on with string.

**6.** Observe the snails' behavior for 2 or 3 days to find out what they prefer to eat. Even if you don't see them munching, you can see which type of food is disappearing. The snails leave another clue . . . a telltale trail of slime. Remember to keep the paper towel moist.

**7.** After a few days, release the snails in a cool, moist area.

ACTION, REACTION, RESULTS

Snails belong to a large group of mollusks called gastropods. Gastropod means "stomach-foot." The name comes from the fact that they glide along on a large single "foot" that appears to be under the stomach of the creature. Land snails such as the common brown garden snail make a shiny trail of slime that helps them to move over surfaces more easily. Many snails, including the garden snail, eat plant matter with a raspy "tongue" called a radula.

**WORD FILE**

**Habitat:** A place where a plant or animal lives.

**Mollusk:** A group of soft-bodied animals without a backbone. Many mollusks are protected by a hard shell and live either in water or damp places.

# ANY WAY THE WIND BLOWS

*Do you ever wonder about the weather?*
*This wind sock can be one of the tools to help you keep track*
*of the weather in a backyard weather station.*

**Setup time:** 30 minutes ● **Observation time:** ongoing, when wind blows

## MATERIALS

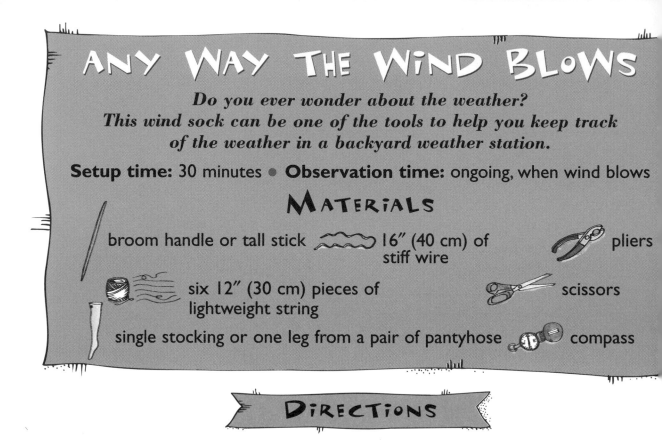

broom handle or tall stick

16" (40 cm) of stiff wire

pliers

six 12" (30 cm) pieces of lightweight string

scissors

single stocking or one leg from a pair of pantyhose

compass

## DIRECTIONS

**1.** Secure the broom handle or stick in the ground so that it stands up straight and will not tip over.

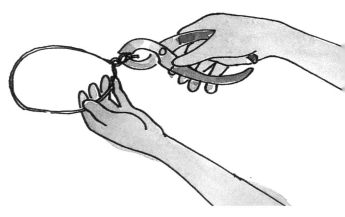

**2.** Create a loop with the stiff wire and use the pliers to twist the ends together.

**3.** Use the scissors to poke six evenly spaced holes near the open end of the stocking. Place the open end of the stocking over the wire. Thread one end of each string through a hole and around the wire, then tie it in place.

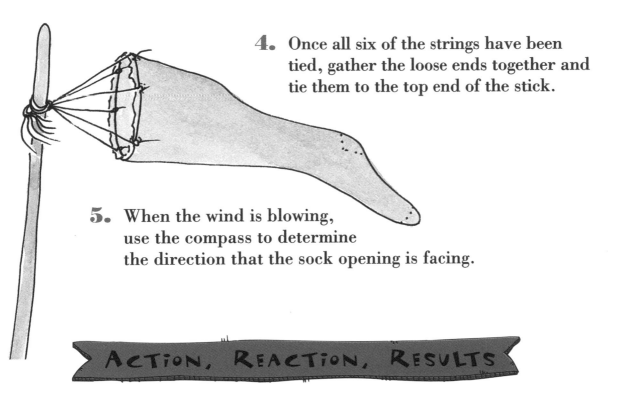

4. Once all six of the strings have been tied, gather the loose ends together and tie them to the top end of the stick.

5. When the wind is blowing, use the compass to determine the direction that the sock opening is facing.

## ACTION, REACTION, RESULTS

The wind blows into the open end of the sock. The toe points in the direction that the wind is blowing. The direction that the opening is facing names the wind. Wind blowing from north to south is called a north wind. You can tell how strong the wind is by how straight the wind sock is.

> Wind direction is very important to people who fly planes and sail boats. You will often see wind socks at airports and seaports.

# DOWN WITH DETERGENTS

*People use detergents to clean many things—everything from clothes and dishes to cars. Dishwashing liquid is a common household detergent. You might be surprised to find that in the wrong places, detergent has a downside.*

**Setup time:** 5 minutes ● **Observation time:** 5 minutes

## MATERIALS

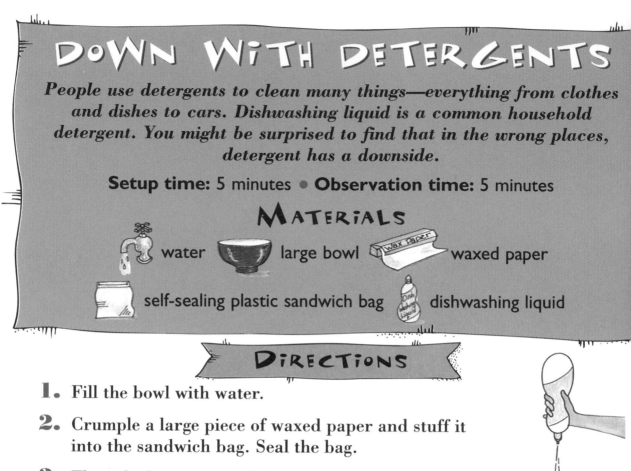

water ● large bowl ● waxed paper ● self-sealing plastic sandwich bag ● dishwashing liquid

## DIRECTIONS

**1.** Fill the bowl with water.

**2.** Crumple a large piece of waxed paper and stuff it into the sandwich bag. Seal the bag.

**3.** Float the bag on top of the water. Add several big squirts of dishwashing liquid to the water and observe. Does the bag begin to sink?

## ACTION, REACTION, RESULTS

**WORD FILE**

**Detergent:** A chemical substance used to remove dirt, oil, and grease from other materials.

One reason that the bag floats on the surface of the water is because it has an oily coating that makes it water repellent. Detergent in the dishwashing liquid breaks up the oily coating, and the bag begins to sink.

If detergents enter a natural water supply, they can cause harm to wildlife. For example, water birds rely on their water repellent feathers to float, and detergents can make their feathers less water repellent. When hiking or camping, it is important not to use detergents in or near lakes, rivers, ponds, or streams.

# NO SWEAT

*Some days feel dry and crisp. Others feel damp and muggy. The difference is due to differences in the humidity. You can build your own simple psychrometer to tell whether the humidity is high or low.*

**Setup time:** 30 minutes • **Observation time:** 15 minutes, then ongoing

## MATERIALS

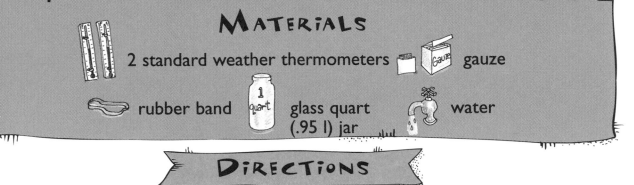

2 standard weather thermometers    gauze

rubber band    glass quart (.95 l) jar    water

## DIRECTIONS

**1.** Wrap the base of one thermometer in several layers of gauze. Secure the gauze with a rubber band.

**2.** Fill the jar with water. Place the gauze-wrapped thermometer in the jar so that the bulb is submerged.

**3.** Place the jar and the other thermometer outside in an area out of direct sunlight. Wait 15 minutes, then compare the temperatures between the two thermometers.

15 minutes

**4.** Keep water in the jar and compare the temperatures daily.

## ACTION, REACTION, RESULTS

Humidity is measured by comparing the temperature between the two thermometers. The temperature of the wet thermometer will always be lower than the dry one. The greater the difference between the two, the lower the humidity.

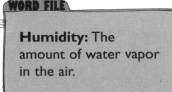

**WORD FILE**

**Humidity:** The amount of water vapor in the air.

# WONDERFUL WATER

*Plants need sunlight, air, water, and soil to grow.*
*Will they still grow if you leave out the soil? Give it a try.*

**Setup time:** 20 minutes ● **Observation time:** ongoing, once a day

## MATERIALS

pebbles     shallow baking dish     water

3 clay flower pots     peat moss

flower seeds     liquid plant food     spray bottle

## DIRECTIONS

1. In a sunny window, place a layer of pebbles in the baking dish. Fill each pot with peat moss and set the pots on the pebbles.

2. Scatter several seeds in each pot, then press down the peat moss.

3. Fill the baking dish with water. The water level should be even with the bottom of the pots. Using the spray bottle filled with water, moisten the peat moss so that it is damp but not soaked.

Hydroponics

4. Check the water level in the baking dish every day, and fill to the bottom of the pots when necessary. Spray the peat moss so that it remains moist.

5. Once the seeds germinate, once a week add liquid plant food to the spray bottle according to directions on the plant food.

## ACTION, REACTION, RESULTS

Plants need certain things to grow. They use sunlight, water, and air to make their own food through photosynthesis. Plants also need minerals that they usually get from the soil. Peat moss holds water well, but it doesn't have the same nutrients as soil. By using liquid plant food in the water, you provide the minerals they need.

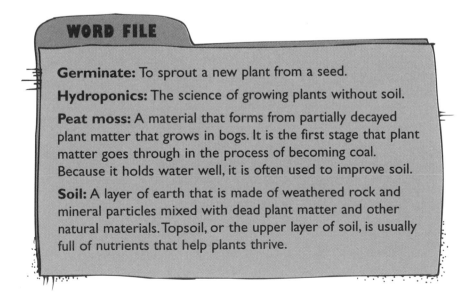

**WORD FILE**

**Germinate:** To sprout a new plant from a seed.

**Hydroponics:** The science of growing plants without soil.

**Peat moss:** A material that forms from partially decayed plant matter that grows in bogs. It is the first stage that plant matter goes through in the process of becoming coal. Because it holds water well, it is often used to improve soil.

**Soil:** A layer of earth that is made of weathered rock and mineral particles mixed with dead plant matter and other natural materials. Topsoil, or the upper layer of soil, is usually full of nutrients that help plants thrive.

# SOIL'S SECRET

*The soil beneath your feet may feel very firm,*
*but you don't have to go far to find the water in it.*

**Setup time:** 15 minutes ● **Observation time:** 2 hours

## MATERIALS

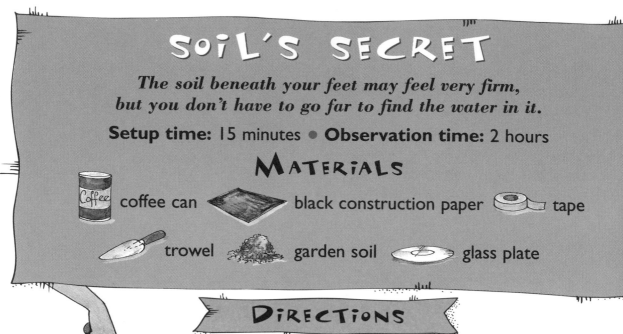

coffee can • black construction paper • tape • trowel • garden soil • glass plate

## DIRECTIONS

1. Cover the outside of the coffee can with black construction paper and tape it in place.

2. Fill the can to within 2" (5 cm) of the edge with soil from your garden.

3. Cover the top of the can with the glass plate and place it in a sunny location for 2 hours. Check the bottom of the plate for moisture.

2 hours

## ACTION, REACTION, RESULTS

**WORD FILE**

**Condense:** To change from a vapor state to a liquid state or a more solid state.

**Evaporate:** To convert, or change, into vapor.

You will find some moisture in most types of soil. In this experiment, the warmth of the sun causes the water in your soil sample to evaporate, then condense on the plate. Try different types of soil to see which contains the most moisture.

Soil Characteristics

# TEA GARDEN

*If there is a tea drinker in your family,*
*you have the fixings for a minigarden in every leftover tea bag.*

**Setup time:** 10 minutes • **Observation time:** 3 weeks

## MATERIALS

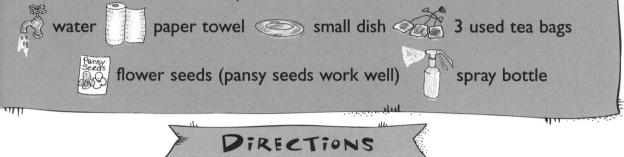

water    paper towel    small dish    3 used tea bags

flower seeds (pansy seeds work well)    spray bottle

## DIRECTIONS

**1.** Wet the paper towel, fold it in half, and lay it on the dish.

**2.** Soak the used tea bags, then lay them on top of the towel.

**3.** Make a hole in the center of the tea bags and poke a seed or two inside each bag.

**4.** Place the dish in a warm, sunny location. Check it every day. Mist the tea bags and towel with water to keep them damp, but not soaking wet. One or more plants should sprout within 2 weeks. When the plants are about 2″ (5 cm) high, plant the tea bags directly into garden soil.

## ACTION, REACTION, RESULTS

As long as it is kept warm and moist, a seed can germinate. Much of what a new plant needs to survive is in the seed. When nutrients in the seed are used up, the tiny plant can get food from the tea bag. Tea is made from the leaves of a plant, and the leaves contain important nutrients.

**WORD FILE**

**Germinate:** To start to grow.

**Nutrient:** A substance used to feed a living organism.

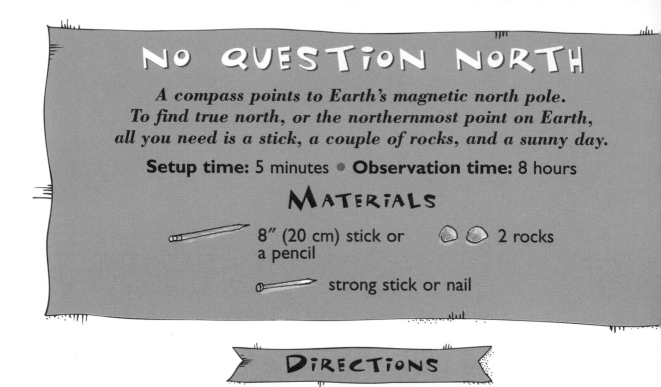

# NO QUESTION NORTH

*A compass points to Earth's magnetic north pole.*
*To find true north, or the northernmost point on Earth,*
*all you need is a stick, a couple of rocks, and a sunny day.*

**Setup time:** 5 minutes • **Observation time:** 8 hours

## MATERIALS

8" (20 cm) stick or a pencil

2 rocks

strong stick or nail

## DIRECTIONS

**1.** At about nine o'clock in the morning in a sunny location, push a pencil or stick in the ground so that it stands straight up.

**2.** Starting at the tip of the pencil's shadow and using the nail or strong stick, draw a circle around the pencil. Keep your circle line the same distance from the pencil as the length of the shadow. Make it as round as possible. Place a rock where the shadow touches the circle.

**30**

**3.** Check your setup throughout the day. As time passes, the shadow will become shorter, then longer again. Once it touches the circle again, mark the spot with a rock. Draw a straight line to connect the two rocks.

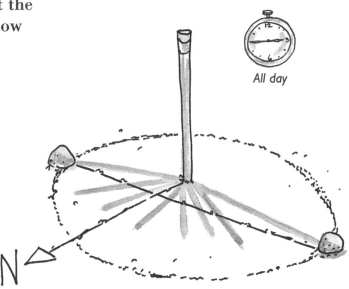

All day

**4.** Draw a line from the pencil to the center of the line that connects the rocks. That line will point to true north.

N

ACTION, REACTION, RESULTS

The sun appears to move across the sky from east to west. The line you draw from rock to rock in this experiment is an east to west line. In the northern hemisphere, a line drawn from the pencil to the center of the east-west line will always point to the geographic north pole, or true north.

**WORD FILE**

**Hemisphere:** Half of a round or ball-shaped object. The equator is an imaginary line that runs around the middle of the planet. The northern hemisphere is that half of the Earth that is north of the equator.

The magnetic poles are different from the geographic poles. The Earth is surrounded by a magnetic field. The magnetic poles are the two points where this field comes in contact with the Earth. A compass needle points to magnetic north. After taking a compass reading, navigators adjust their findings to true north, which helps them to figure out where they are.

# A CHANGE IN THE WEATHER

*Have you ever made plans to do something outside, only to have to change your plans because of unexpected bad weather? Other instruments you might use in a backyard weather station mostly help you observe the weather, but this barometer will help you predict upcoming changes.*

**Setup time:** 20 minutes ● **Observation time:** ongoing, once a day

## MATERIALS

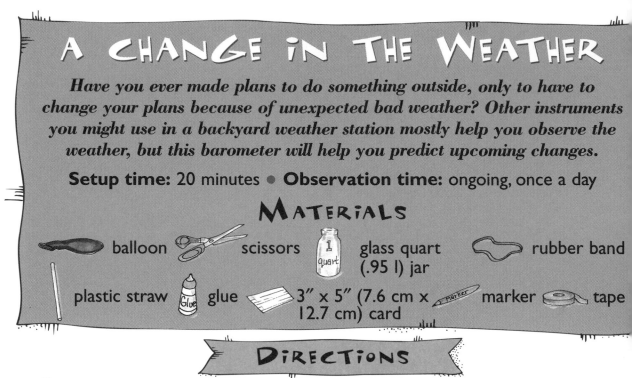

balloon · scissors · glass quart (.95 l) jar · rubber band

plastic straw · glue · 3" x 5" (7.6 cm x 12.7 cm) card · marker · tape

## DIRECTIONS

**1.** Cut a piece of balloon large enough to fit loosely over the top of the jar. Secure it in place with a rubber band.

**2.** Cut a piece of straw 6" (15 cm) long. Glue one end of the straw horizontally to the center of the balloon material. Place the jar on a flat surface in a sheltered area near a wall.

**3.** Holding the card lengthwise, write "HIGH" on the top and "LOW" on the bottom. Draw a horizontal line across the middle. Tape the card to the wall so that the straw is centered exactly on the line between the two words.

**4.** Check your barometer regularly, once a day. Does the straw move? If the straw is above the line, the weather is likely to be clear. If it is below the line, cloudy or stormy weather is in store.

## ACTION, REACTION, RESULTS

A barometer is used to measure air pressure and to predict changes in the weather. When air pressure is high the air pushes down on the balloon causing the straw to move above the line. When the air pressure is low, the straw will move below the line. High pressure usually indicates clear, stable weather. Low pressure indicates a storm or change.

Air Pressure

# DOWN THE DRAIN

*The rain forest is filled with lush plants, so you might think that it has nutrient-rich soil. In fact, rain forest soil has few nutrients. This experiment demonstrates one reason why.*

**Setup time:** 15 minutes • **Observation time:** 20 minutes

## MATERIALS

funnel   4 coffee filters   glass quart (.95 l) jar   1 cup of soil

½ teaspoon of powdered green paint (available at art supply stores)

water   measuring cup   4 plastic glasses

## DIRECTIONS

1. Place a coffee filter in the funnel and set the funnel atop the glass jar.

2. Fill the filter with soil and mix in the powdered paint.

3. Pour ¾ cup (175 ml) of tap water through the soil. Once it has drained through, pour it from the jar into a plastic glass.

4. Repeat step 3 three more times. Is the colored water in each glass the same shade of green?

## ACTION, REACTION, RESULTS

In this experiment, the green paint represents nutrients in the soil. The water represents the rain from a downpour. Each time it "rains," "nutrients" are washed away. If you continue to pour water through the soil, all of the nutrients (represented by green paint) will eventually drain away and the water will be clear.

**WORD FILE**

**Nutrients:** Substances that provide food for a living thing.

**Rain forest:** An evergreen forest that has abundant rainfall throughout the year.

# NUMBER THE STARS

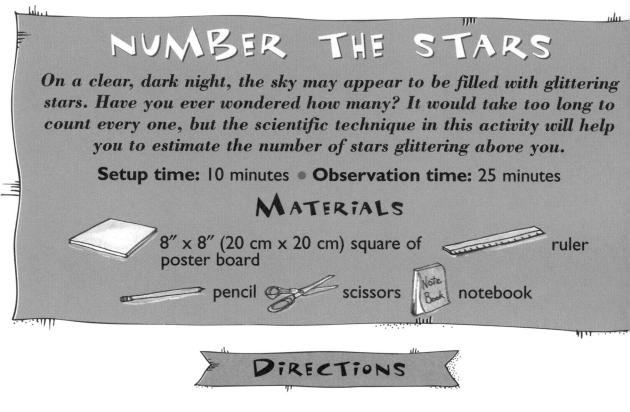

*On a clear, dark night, the sky may appear to be filled with glittering stars. Have you ever wondered how many? It would take too long to count every one, but the scientific technique in this activity will help you to estimate the number of stars glittering above you.*

**Setup time:** 10 minutes ● **Observation time:** 25 minutes

## MATERIALS

8″ x 8″ (20 cm x 20 cm) square of poster board     ruler

pencil     scissors     notebook

## DIRECTIONS

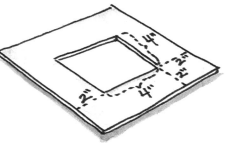

**1.** Place the poster board on a flat surface. Measure and cut a 4″ x 4″ (10 cm x 10 cm) square from the center. You will have a square frame that is 2″ (5 cm) wide on each side.

**2.** Go outside and wait 5 minutes until your eyes adjust to the dark. Close one eye. Hold the frame 12″ (30 cm) from your open eye and count all of the stars you can see within the square. Be sure to hold your head and hand still. Record the number in your notebook.

**3.** Repeat your count in 10 different parts of the sky. Record each count in your notebook.

**4.** Add up all 10 numbers, then divide by 10 to get the average number of stars per viewing. Multiply that number by 56. The result will be an estimation of the total number of stars visible in the sky with the naked eye.

ACTION, REACTION, RESULTS

A square 4″ (10 cm) on each side held 12″ (30 cm) from your eye, gives you a view of approximately ¹⁄₅₆ of the celestial hemisphere. First you find the average number of stars that may be visible in the square by taking 10 different samplings, then multiply to find the total. How do you know you are seeing ¹⁄₅₆ at a time? At a distance of 12″ (30 cm) from your eye, the total surface of the celestial hemisphere is about 905 sq. in. (5,837 cm²). The frame allows you to view 16 sq. in. (103 cm²) at a time (905 divided by 16 = 56; 5,837 divided by 103 = 56).

**WORD FILE**

**Average:** Typical or in the middle. A mathematical average is the result of dividing the sum by the number of items added to total that sum.

**Celestial** hemisphere: The domelike view an earthling has of the night sky.

**Estimate:** To figure out roughly or approximately.

**Surface area:** The measure of a surface in square units of length, such as square feet or inches.

# EARTHWORKS

*Have you ever seen a natural cave, one that wasn't man-made? Natural caves can form in different ways, but limestone caves are carved out through the erosive action of water.*

**Setup time:** 5 minutes • **Observation time:** 30 minutes

## MATERIALS

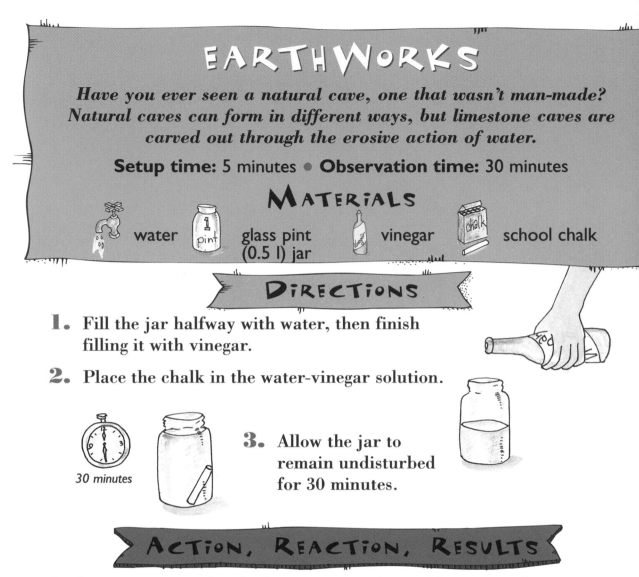

water • glass pint (0.5 l) jar • vinegar • school chalk

## DIRECTIONS

**1.** Fill the jar halfway with water, then finish filling it with vinegar.

**2.** Place the chalk in the water-vinegar solution.

*30 minutes*

**3.** Allow the jar to remain undisturbed for 30 minutes.

## ACTION, REACTION, RESULTS

In this experiment, the chalk you use is a form of limestone. Limestone is a sedimentary rock formed on shallow seabeds. It is made up of calcium carbonate, mainly small particles of seashells. Limestone is comparatively soft. The water and vinegar represents rainwater, which is slightly acidic. It dissolves the chalk. A similar process happens when rainwater seeps through underground beds of limestone. Where rainwater flows and pools, it gradually dissolves areas of the limestone, and those areas become caves.

**WORD FILE**

**Acidic:** Having the properties of an acid or producing an acid.

**Erosive:** The tendency of one substance to wear away another.

**Sedimentary rock:** Rock formed by the settling of particles that form layers and harden due to the pressure of the layers above.

**36**

# ON TARGET

*Hitting a moving target can be difficult. In this experiment, you'll try to hit a target that is standing still while you are moving.*

**Setup time:** 10 minutes • **Observation time:** 10 minutes

## MATERIALS

old sock • playground sand • flat rock

## DIRECTIONS

**1.** Partially fill the sock with sand and tie a knot in it.

**2.** Place the rock on the ground for a target. Stand about 20′ (6 m) from the target.

**3.** Hold the sock out to one side and run as fast as you can past the target. Try to drop the sock directly on the target as you pass.

**WORD FILE**

**Momentum:** The force produced by a moving body.

## ACTION, REACTION, RESULTS

The sock does not drop down in a straight line. Because you are moving when you drop the sock, it has some forward motion, or momentum. It falls in a curved path and lands in front of the target.

# RAIN RATES

*A backyard weather station wouldn't be complete without a rain gauge. A simple rain gauge will help you keep track of how much rain each storm brings. Over time you can figure out the rainiest months of the year.*

**Setup time:** 30 minutes ● **Observation time:** ongoing, daily

## MATERIALS

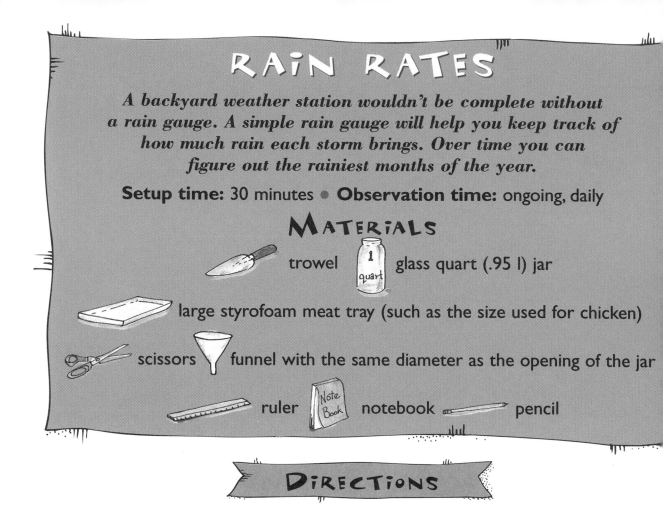

trowel    glass quart (.95 l) jar

large styrofoam meat tray (such as the size used for chicken)

scissors    funnel with the same diameter as the opening of the jar

ruler    notebook    pencil

## DIRECTIONS

**1.** In an open area free from overhanging plants or other obstructions, where it's okay to dig, dig a hole as deep as the jar is high but wide enough so the jar can be easily moved in and out.

**2.** Place the jar in the hole. The neck of the jar should be even with the soil level.

Measuring Rainfall

**3.** Cover the opening to the hole with the styrofoam tray. Cut a hole in the center of the tray just large enough to fit the funnel spout. Stick the spout through the hole.

**4.** Check the jar at the same time every 24 hours for a month. Take the jar out of the hole. If there is any collected water, use the ruler to measure in inches how deep it is. Record the amount in your notebook, dump out the water, then replace the jar, tray, and funnel.

ACTION, REACTION, RESULTS

This simple rain gauge does not measure actual rainfall in inches (centimeters). It is a way of comparing total rainfall over days or months. Over time, you can predict a pattern. A standard rain gauge is an instrument with an open-topped container that has been calibrated (filled with fluid, measured, and marked) so the amount of rain that falls into it can be accurately measured.

**WORD FILE**

**Funnel:** An object used to pour a substance into a narrow-necked container. It has a wide mouth at the top and a narrow spout at the bottom.

**Gauge:** A measuring instrument.

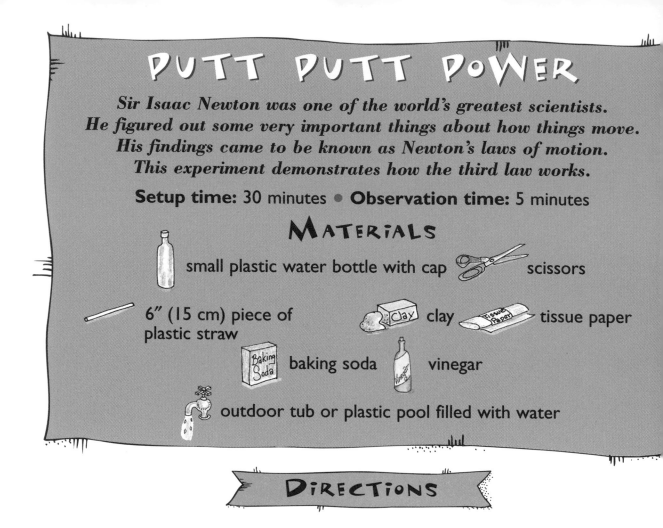

# PUTT PUTT POWER

*Sir Isaac Newton was one of the world's greatest scientists.*
*He figured out some very important things about how things move.*
*His findings came to be known as Newton's laws of motion.*
*This experiment demonstrates how the third law works.*

**Setup time:** 30 minutes • **Observation time:** 5 minutes

## MATERIALS

small plastic water bottle with cap — scissors

6" (15 cm) piece of plastic straw — clay — tissue paper

baking soda — vinegar

outdoor tub or plastic pool filled with water

## DIRECTIONS

**1.** Ask an adult helper to use the scissors or a knife to make a hole large enough to hold the straw near one edge in the base of the bottle.

**2.** Slip the straw into the hole and leave about 1" (2.5 cm) sticking out at the bottom. Seal the edges around the straw with clay.

**3.** Tear a piece of tissue about 2" (5 cm) square. Place about a tablespoon of baking soda on the tissue, roll the tissue to enclose the soda, and twist the ends closed.

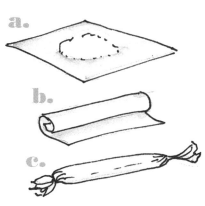

a.
b.
c.

Newton's Third Law, Chemical Reaction

**4.** Fill the bottle halfway with vinegar. Slip the filled tissue into the bottle and quickly put on the cap. Moving quickly, place the bottle on its side in the tub of water so that the straw is submerged. Let go and let your "boat" take off.

## ACTION, REACTION, RESULTS

The baking soda and vinegar combine in a chemical reaction that produces carbon dioxide gas. The gas expands inside the bottle and escapes through the straw. The gas escapes in one direction which forces the bottle in the other direction. This demonstration is an example of Newton's third law of motion which states that every action has an equal and opposite reaction.

**WORD FILE**

**Chemical reaction:** The interaction of two or more substances that brings about a chemical change in them.

**Submerge:** To put a solid object in water so that it is covered.

# A RECIPE FOR DIRT

*Not all soil is the same. Some soils hold water and dry out slowly, and others drain and dry out quickly. Knowing the type of soil you have can help you make your garden grow better.*

**Setup time:** 30 minutes • **Observation time:** 8 hours

## MATERIALS

trowel    3 glass pint (0.5 l) jars with lids    3 stick-on labels

water    marker    notebook    soil

kitchen bulb siphon or turkey baster    magnifying glass

## DIRECTIONS

**1.** Fill each jar with 2″ (5 cm) of soil. Collect each sample from a different part of your neighborhood. Label each jar and write where the sample came from. In your notebook, jot down information about the types of plants and any animals that lived in the sample area.

**2.** Fill each jar with water, put on the lid, and shake until the soil is mixed. Leave the jars undisturbed for an hour or until all of the soil has settled. Note which jar settled first. Look for layers.

*I hour*

Soil Composition

**3.** Siphon out as much water as you can from each jar. Without shaking or disturbing the soil, set the jars in a sunny spot with the lids off so that the water will evaporate. Once the soil is dry, use the magnifying glass to examine the differences between the layers.

## ACTION, REACTION, RESULTS

Soil is formed from many elements including weathered rock and minerals. The type of soil it is depends on the original rock, climate, rainfall, and even the plants in the area. In this experiment, the soil becomes mixed with water, and as it settles, the heavier elements settle first and the lighter ones settle last forming layers. There are four basic kinds of soil: clay, sand, silt, and loam. Clay is the heaviest; loam is the lightest.

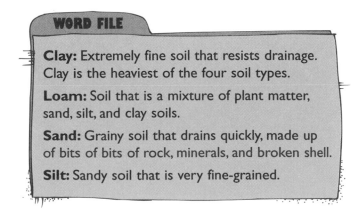

**WORD FILE**

**Clay:** Extremely fine soil that resists drainage. Clay is the heaviest of the four soil types.

**Loam:** Soil that is a mixture of plant matter, sand, silt, and clay soils.

**Sand:** Grainy soil that drains quickly, made up of bits of bits of rock, minerals, and broken shell.

**Silt:** Sandy soil that is very fine-grained.

# LET IT SNOW

*A cold, snowy day may not seem like a good time to be outside, but it's perfect for this experiment.*

**Setup time:** 24 hours • **Observation time:** 1 hour

## MATERIALS

3" x 5" (7.6 cm x 12.7 cm) piece of glass from a photo frame

clear spray lacquer (available at hardware stores)　rubber gloves

tweezers　　magnifying glass　　refrigerator and freezer

## DIRECTIONS

**1.** On the night before snow is predicted, place the glass in the freezer. Put the can of lacquer and tweezers in the refrigerator.

**2.** Later when it's snowing, wear rubber gloves and use tweezers to remove the glass from the freezer. Using newspaper to protect anything that might get accidently sprayed, spray a layer of lacquer on the glass. Place the glass in an open area outside where snow is falling.

**3.** After about 5 minutes, move the glass to a cold but protected area. Let it remain undisturbed for 1 hour.

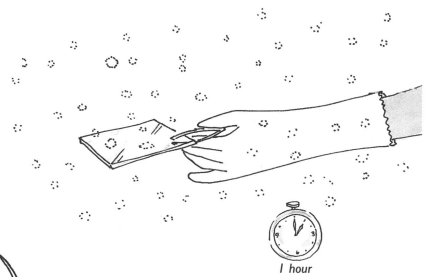

I hour

**4.** Bring the glass inside. Use the magnifying glass to study the patterns of the snowflakes.

ACTION, REACTION, RESULTS

What you see on the glass in this experiment are impressions of the snowflakes preserved in the dry lacquer. This method allows you to study the patterns even inside your warm house. Snowflakes are ice crystals that form from water vapor in clouds. The crystals take many forms, but they are always six-sided. No two snowflakes are alike.

**WORD FILE**

**Crystals:** A clear solid substance with flat surfaces that meet at regular angles and form regular shapes.

**Pattern:** A natural shape, design, or configuration.

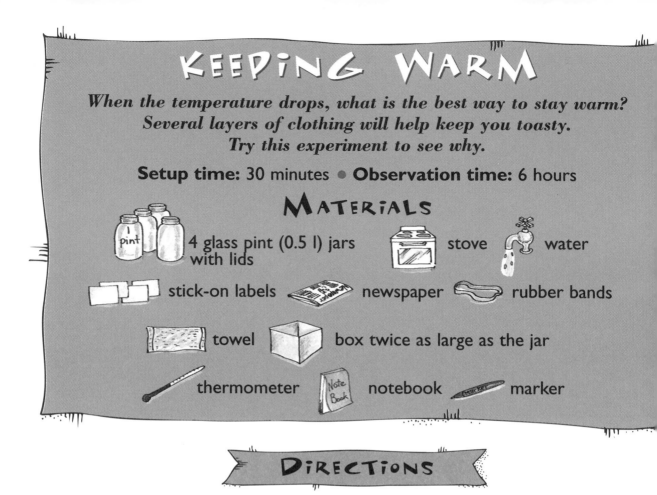

# KEEPING WARM

*When the temperature drops, what is the best way to stay warm?*
*Several layers of clothing will help keep you toasty.*
*Try this experiment to see why.*

**Setup time:** 30 minutes • **Observation time:** 6 hours

## MATERIALS

4 glass pint (0.5 l) jars with lids — stove — water

stick-on labels — newspaper — rubber bands

towel — box twice as large as the jar

thermometer — notebook — marker

## DIRECTIONS

**1.** Ask an adult helper to boil 4 cups (1,000 ml) of water for you. Fill each of the four jars half-full with the hot water and put on the lids. Label and number each jar.

**2.** Wrap jar 1 with a thick layer of newspaper and secure it with rubber bands. Be sure to cover the top and bottom, too.

Jar 1    Jar 2    Jar 3

Jar 4

*30 minutes*

**3.** Wrap jar 2 completely in a towel.

**4.** Place jar 3 in the box. Stuff crumpled newspaper firmly all around it. Leave jar 4 out in the open.

**5.** After ½ hour, check the temperature in each jar and write it in your notebook.

**6.** Check each jar every ½ hour until the water in each has reached room temperature. Which jar took the longest to reach room temperature?

ACTION, REACTION, RESULTS

In this experiment, the jar left in the open loses heat more quickly than the others. Insulation prevents heat or cold from draining away. Some materials are good insulators and conserve heat or cold well.

Layers of air within or between materials improve the efficiency of the insulation. When you are going to spend time outside in cold weather, wearing layers of clothing will keep you warmer.

# EARTH TO STAR

*Early sailors used an astrolabe to determine their location at sea. If you make one of your own, the stars can tell you where you are on the Earth.*

**Setup time:** 20 minutes • **Observation time:** 10 minutes

## MATERIALS

plastic protractor (from a stationery store)

metal nut (the kind that goes on a bolt)

pencil    string    scissors

## DIRECTIONS

**1.** Measure the protractor from the flat side across to the far edge of the rounded side. Cut a piece of string double that length. Tie one end of the string to the nut. Tie the other end to the center of the flat side of the protractor.

**2.** Cut two short pieces of string and use them to tie the pencil against the flat, unnumbered side of the protractor.

**48**

**3.** On a clear night, hold the pencil up to one eye and look along it to get a good line of sight. Point the tip of the pencil at the North Star. Hold the instrument in place and look at the side of the astrolabe to get a reading. The weighted string will be in line with the number, or degree, of your latitude.

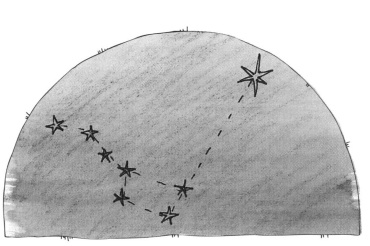

## ACTION, REACTION, RESULTS

People use latitude lines to figure out how far north or south they are of the equator. The protractor you used to make your astrolabe is used to measure angles. When you point the pencil at the North Star, the string measures the angle between the North Star and the horizon.

**WORD FILE**

**Equator:** An imaginary line around the center of the Earth usually identified on maps.

**Latitude:** A series of imaginary lines running east and west around the Earth and often identified on maps.

# QUICK QUICKSAND

*Can you imagine ground that looks like a solid but acts like a fluid? You don't have to imagine. With this demonstration of a non-Newtonian fluid you can create your own backyard quicksand.*

**Setup time:** 10 minutes • **Observation time:** 10 minutes

## MATERIALS

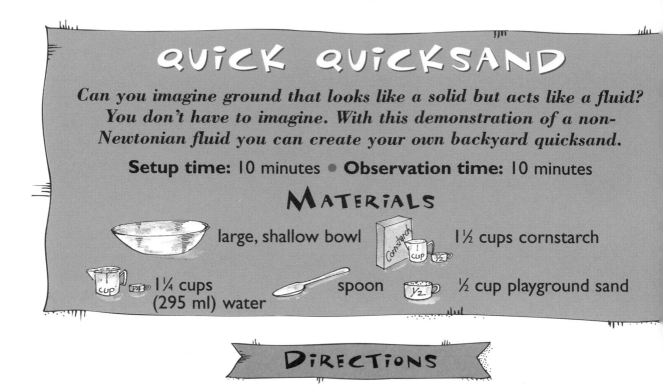

large, shallow bowl

1½ cups cornstarch

1¼ cups (295 ml) water

spoon

½ cup playground sand

## DIRECTIONS

**1.** Mix cornstarch and water in the bowl. It should be like thick mud, a little hard to stir but not dry. You may need to adjust the mixture to get the right texture.

**2.** Sprinkle the surface of the mixture with playground sand.

**3.** With two fingers, press lightly on the surface. Do your fingers sink easily into the mixture as they would in a fluid? Try striking it hard with your fist. Does the mixture resist like a solid?

Non-Newtonian Fluid

The cornstarch mixture is a non-Newtonian fluid. Fluids have a property called viscosity, or resistance to flow. A fluid with high viscosity, like honey, flows slowly. A fluid with low viscosity, like water, flows quickly. The viscosity of a non-Newtonian fluid can be changed by applying a force. In this experiment, when you press gently, you are applying little force and the fluid is less viscous. Your fingers sink in. When you hit the surface with greater force, the fluid becomes more viscous, and for a short time, acts more like a solid. Your fist meets resistance.

**WORD FILE**

**Fluid:** A substance that flows and takes the shape of the container it is in.

**Force:** Energy that can be measured by its effect. A force is anything that can stop or start an object, change its direction, or change its shape.

**Solid:** A substance that does not flow and retains its own size and shape.

In this demonstration, the grains of cornstarch are suspended in water. Real quicksand is a bed of sand saturated by upwardly flowing water. The grains of sand shift and yield easily to pressure.

# FOUNTAIN FUN

*Create a fountain for your own backyard using warm water and air pressure.*

**Setup time:** 30 minutes • **Observation time:** 15 minutes

## MATERIALS

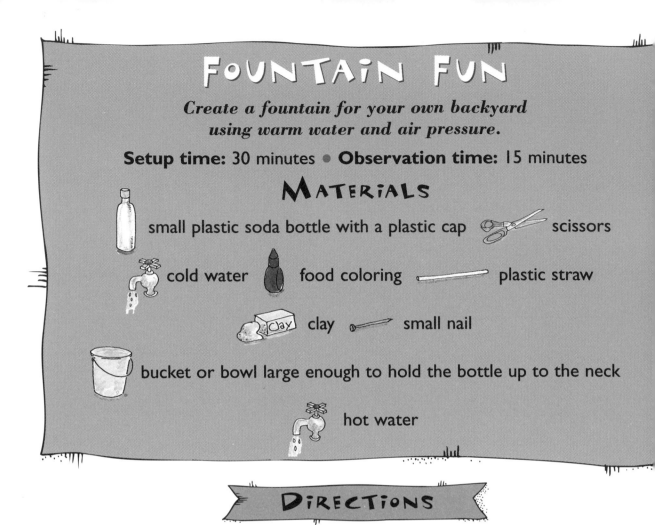

small plastic soda bottle with a plastic cap   scissors

cold water   food coloring   plastic straw

clay   small nail

bucket or bowl large enough to hold the bottle up to the neck

hot water

## DIRECTIONS

**1.** Get an adult helper to use scissors or a small knife to poke a hole in the bottle cap large enough to push the straw through. Fill the bottle halfway with cold water. Add a few drops of food coloring. Put on the cap.

**2.** Push the straw through the hole in the cap so that the end of the straw is about an inch from the bottom of the bottle. Surround the hole with clay to seal it.

**3.** Fill the top of the straw with clay to create a plug. Use the nail to make a small hole through the clay plug.

**4.** Place the bottle in a bucket or bowl. Ask an adult to fill the bucket with very hot water. Wait for a while. What happens when the water in the bottle warms up?

## ACTION, REACTION, RESULTS

The air in the bottle is cold, and that means that the air molecules have moved closer together. The air contracted. When you add hot water to the outer bucket, you warm the air in the bottle. The molecules move farther apart and the air expands. The expanding air pushes down on the water in the bottle and forces the water up the straw and out of the tiny opening at the top as a fine spray.

**WORD FILE**

**Contract:** To squeeze down or get smaller.

**Expand:** To spread out, swell, or get larger.

# DiRECTiON REFLECTiON

*The wind direction at ground level can be affected by landforms, trees, and buildings. To help you get a better picture of which way the wind is blowing, you can make a nephoscope.*

**Setup time:** 20 minutes • **Observation time:** 10 minutes

## MATERiALS

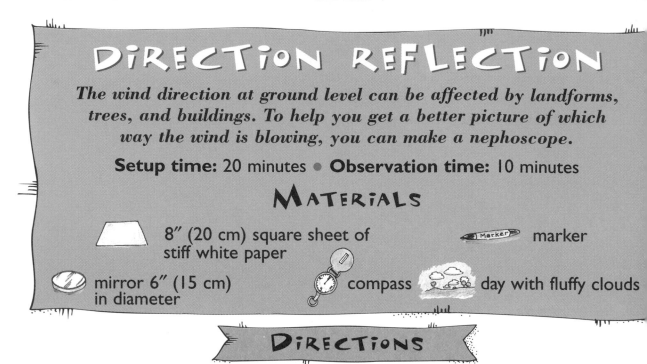

8" (20 cm) square sheet of stiff white paper

mirror 6" (15 cm) in diameter

marker

compass

day with fluffy clouds

## DiRECTiONS

**1.** Mark the top edge of the paper with the letter "N" for north. Mark the left edge "W" for west, the right edge "E" for east, and the bottom edge "S" for south.

**2.** On a day that has fluffy clouds in the sky, place the paper on a flat surface outside. Use a compass to find north and position the paper so that the "N" is to the north.

**3.** Place the mirror in the center of the paper. Look into the mirror and observe the clouds. Are they moving? From what direction?

## ACTiON, REACTiON, RESULTS

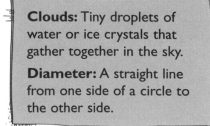

**WORD FILE**

**Clouds:** Tiny droplets of water or ice crystals that gather together in the sky.

**Diameter:** A straight line from one side of a circle to the other side.

As you watch the clouds in your nephoscope, you can determine which direction they are being blown by the wind. This gives you information about the wind direction. The wind is named for the direction the wind is blowing from. For example, a north wind will make the clouds move from north to south across the nephoscope.

Wind Direction

# CHANGING COLORS

*Plants need water to survive. The water must get all the way from the soil to every part of the plant. It does this through little "highways" in the stem called xylem.*

**Setup time:** 15 minutes ● **Observation time:** 1 hour

## MATERIALS

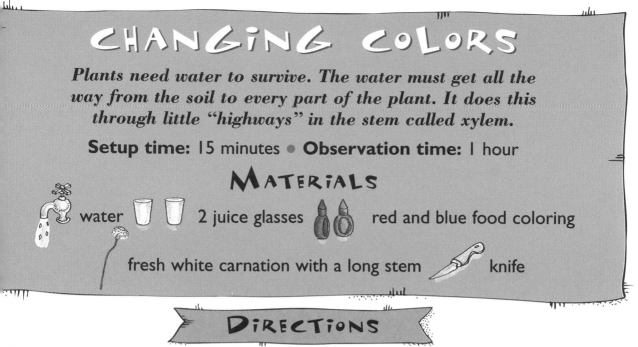

water ● 2 juice glasses ● red and blue food coloring

fresh white carnation with a long stem ● knife

## DIRECTIONS

**1.** Fill one glass with 2″ (5 cm) of water and 10 drops of red food coloring.

**2.** Fill the second glass with about 2″ (5 cm) of water and 10 drops of blue food coloring.

**3.** Have an adult split the stem of the carnation in the middle starting at the bottom and going up for about 3″ (7.5 cm).

**4.** Place the glasses side by side and set the carnation in the glasses so that one part of the stem is in the red water and one part is in the blue water.

**5.** Check the flower after 30 minutes have passed. Check it again after an hour.

*30 minutes
1 hour*

## ACTION, REACTION, RESULTS

The tips of the carnation petals turn colors depending on the color of the water getting to the petals. The food coloring is drawn up the stem in little tubes called xylem that usually carry water and salts from the roots up to the flowers and leaves. Even though the flower has been cut from the plant, the xylem still work. Food substances in the plant are carried from the leaves and down the stem to other parts of the plant through similar tubes called phloem.

# FANTASTIC FUNNEL

*Studying creatures that live in the soil isn't easy unless you can get them to leave their natural environment. A Tullgren funnel is designed to do just that, and this experiment will show you how to make one.*

**Setup time:** 15 minutes ● **Observation time:** 1 hour

## MATERIALS

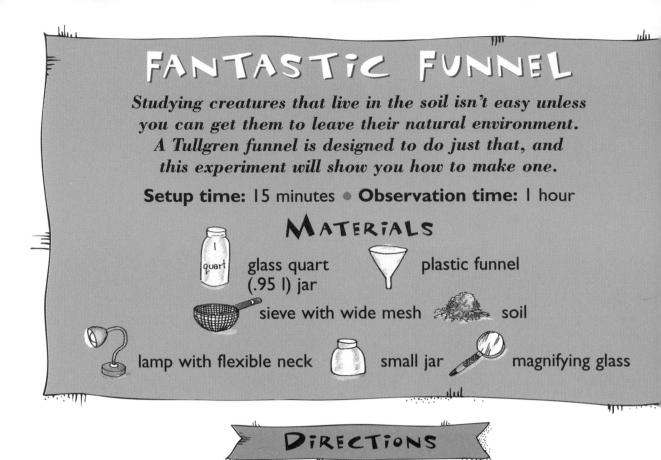

glass quart (.95 l) jar

plastic funnel

sieve with wide mesh

soil

lamp with flexible neck

small jar

magnifying glass

## DIRECTIONS

1. Set the plastic funnel in the quart (.95 l) jar.

2. Place the sieve in the mouth of the funnel and fill it with soil from one location in your yard.

3. Position the lamp over the sieve, but not touching it. Turn on the lamp. Wait for about an hour, then check the jar.

1 hour

56

**4.** Move any creatures you find into a smaller jar so you can study them with the magnifying glass. Use a field guide to help you figure out what the animals are.

**5.** Release the creatures back into the part of the yard where you found them.

## Action, Reaction, Results

Creatures that live in the soil prefer cool, dark conditions. The warmth from the lamp drives them deeper into the soil until they fall through the sieve and into the jar. When you study the insects and other animals that you collect, count how many legs they have. Look for wings, antennae, and other body parts that can help you to identify them with the help of a field guide.

**WORD FILE**

**Antennae:** A pair of long feelers on the head of certain animals such as insects.

**Insect:** An animal with a hard outer skeleton, a three-part body, and three pairs of legs.

# LEFT OR RIGHT

*Are you right or left handed? Can animals be right or left pawed? If you have a cat or dog, or a friend who has a cat or dog, you can find out.*

**Setup time:** 10 minutes • **Observation time:** 5 to 20 minutes

## MATERIALS

clear plastic jar (such as an empty peanut butter jar) • pet treats

masking tape • cooperative pet • notebook • pencil

## DIRECTIONS

**1.** Place a pet treat in the bottom of the jar.

**2.** Put the jar on its side on a flat surface, such as a walkway. Tape down the jar so that it can't be rolled or tipped.

**3.** Show the jar and treat to your pet. Observe which paw the pet uses to try to get the treat out of the jar. Write down your observation.

**4.** Repeat the procedure eight or ten times using the same pet. Record your observations. Reward your pet with a treat for trying.

**5.** Try the experiment with other pets. Record your observations. Remember to reward the pets.

## ACTION, REACTION, RESULTS

**WORD FILE**

**Handedness:** A tendency to use one hand rather than the other.

People tend to favor the use of one hand over another. Most humans are right-handed. Other than the fact that objects are often designed for use with the right hand, there is little benefit of one handedness over the other. Though individuals vary, most animals don't seem to have the same preferences when they try to get the treat. They are often as likely to use the left paw as the right paw to get to a treat.

**58**

# BEFORE AND AFTER

*There are lots of different kinds of pollution, and some you don't have to go outside to find. This is an experiment your parents will probably like.*

**Setup time:** 5 minutes ● **Observation time:** 2 days

## MATERIALS

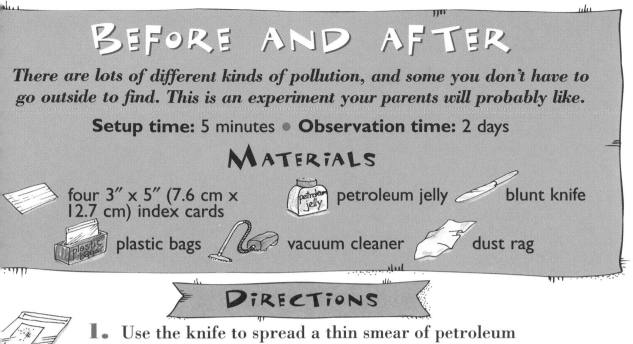

four 3" x 5" (7.6 cm x 12.7 cm) index cards

petroleum jelly

blunt knife

plastic bags

vacuum cleaner

dust rag

## DIRECTIONS

**1.** Use the knife to spread a thin smear of petroleum jelly on two index cards.

**2.** Being careful not to touch the sticky part, place one "pollution trap" on the floor in a place where it won't be disturbed. Place the other on a counter or shelf that is open to the rest of the room.

2 days

**3.** After two days check the cards. Do you see dust and dirt trapped in the petroleum jelly? Place each card in a plastic bag.

**4.** Vacuum your room and dust carefully, then place two new petroleum jelly-covered cards in the same positions as the first.

**5.** After two days, check the cards. Are the results different?

2 days

## ACTION, REACTION, RESULTS

The atmosphere is filled with particles of dust and dirt that are so small they float in the air. The first two cards were exposed to a more "polluted" environment than the second two. By cleaning and vacuuming your room, you remove much of the dust and dirt that is floating around. Without special equipment it is practically impossible to remove all of the particles from the air in your room.

**WORD FILE**

**Dust:** Fine, dry particles of earth or other matter.

**Pollution:** Harmful or unpleasant substances in air, water, or soil.

# SNiP AND CLiP

*Some lawns are long, others are kept clipped short. Is there a point at which a lawn can be mowed too short? This test will help you answer that question and find the growing point of grass.*

**Setup time:** 20 minutes ● **Observation time:** 3 weeks

## MATERiALS

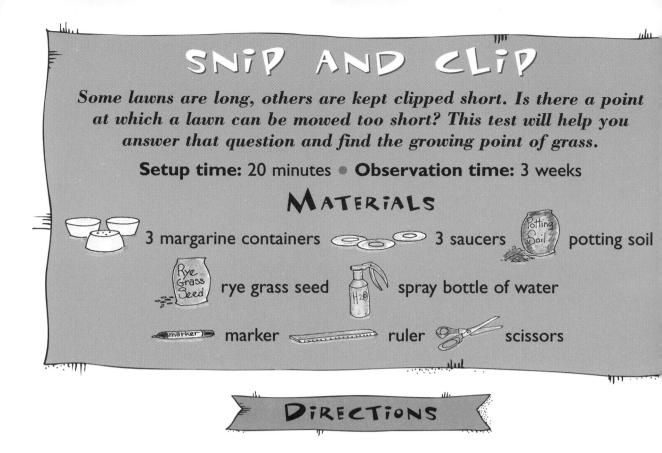

3 margarine containers · 3 saucers · potting soil · rye grass seed · spray bottle of water · marker · ruler · scissors

## DiRECTiONS

1. Ask an adult helper to make several small holes in the bottom of each margarine container.

2. Fill each margarine container to within ½″ (1.5 cm) of the rim with potting soil.

3. Spread a small handful of grass seed evenly on the top of the soil in each container. Top each with another sprinkling of soil so that the seeds are lightly covered. Lightly mist the soil in each container with water.

4. Label each container with a number from one to three.

Growth Point of Plants

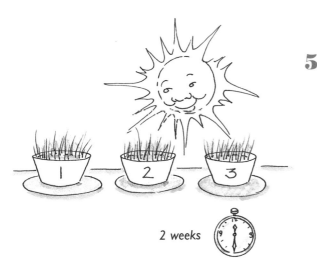

**5.** Place the containers on the saucers in a warm, sunny spot. Check them everyday for two weeks, and use the spray bottle to keep the soil moist.

2 weeks

**6.** After two weeks, measure the length of the grass in each container. Using scissors, cut the grass in the first container by half. Cut the grass in the second container to within ¼″ (0.7 cm) of the soil. Cut the grass in the third container even with the soil.

1 week

**7.** Leave the containers in the same sunny location for one week and keep the soil damp. Did cutting have an effect on the grass?

ACTION, REACTION, RESULTS

Most young plants have a growth point. That is the point at which new leaves are produced. If you cut away the growth point, the plant will die. Rye grass grows from a point at soil level. It can be cropped very short and still survive.

# REACH FOR THE LIGHT

*Plants need light to grow. In this experiment, you will see what great lengths a plant will go to reach light.*

**Setup time:** 30 minutes • **Observation time:** 2 weeks

## MATERIALS

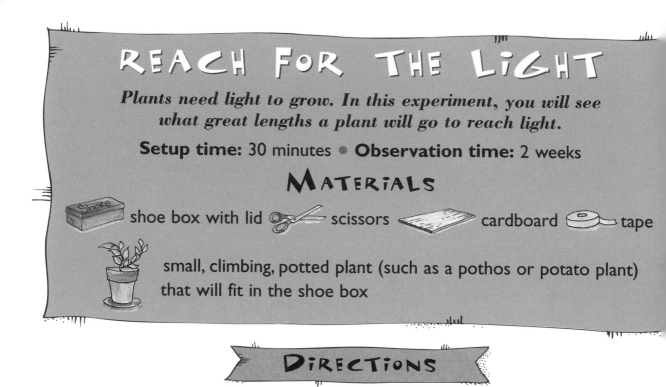

shoe box with lid ✂ scissors ▭ cardboard ◎ tape

small, climbing, potted plant (such as a pothos or potato plant) that will fit in the shoe box

## DIRECTIONS

**1.** Stand the shoe box on one short side so that the length of the box is vertical. Cut a 2″ (5 cm) hole in the top of the box.

**2.** From the cardboard cut two square shelves that are as deep as the shoebox, but 1½″ (3.5 cm) less wide. Cut 2″ (5 cm) wide strips of cardboard to use as shelf braces. Tape the braces and shelves in the box as shown.

To encourage houseplants to grow evenly, it is occasionally necessary to rotate them away from the light source a little at a time.

Phototropism

**3.** Place the box in a sunny location. Make sure the hole is on top. Set the potted plant inside, then close the box with the lid.

**4.** Check the plant every evening for two weeks and water when necessary to keep it moist but not wet. Remember to replace the lid. Does the plant show an unusual growing pattern?

2 weeks

## ACTION, REACTION, RESULTS

Plants need light to fuel the process of photosynthesis. In this experiment, the plant is kept in darkness with one source of light. It grows around the barriers and toward the light.

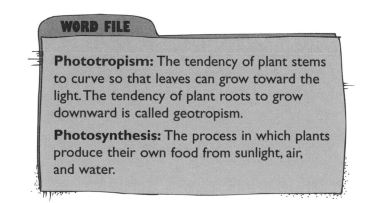

**WORD FILE**

**Phototropism:** The tendency of plant stems to curve so that leaves can grow toward the light. The tendency of plant roots to grow downward is called geotropism.

**Photosynthesis:** The process in which plants produce their own food from sunlight, air, and water.

# VOLCANO

*You probably don't want a real volcano in your backyard, but you can have fun with this small, simple volcano.*

**Setup time:** 30 minutes ● **Observation time:** 5 minutes

## MATERIALS

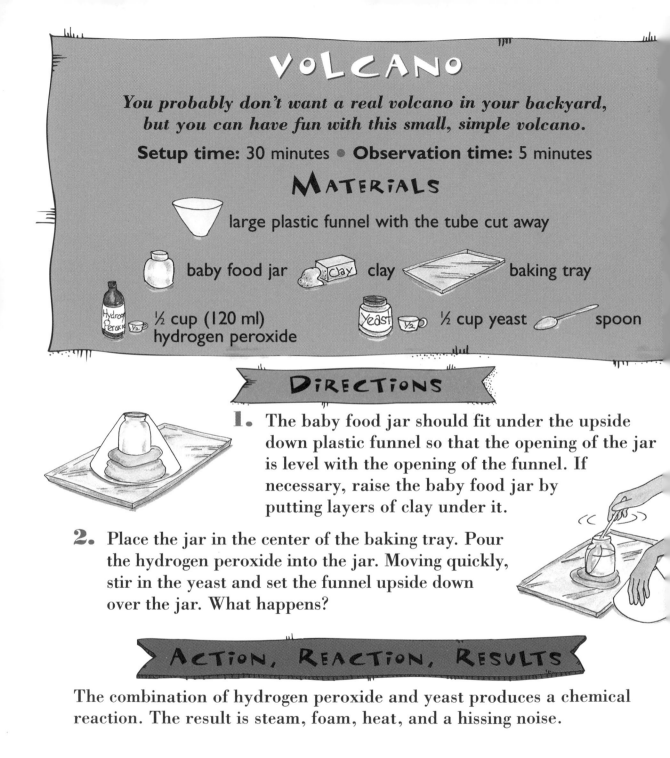

large plastic funnel with the tube cut away

baby food jar     clay     baking tray

½ cup (120 ml) hydrogen peroxide     ½ cup yeast     spoon

## DIRECTIONS

**1.** The baby food jar should fit under the upside down plastic funnel so that the opening of the jar is level with the opening of the funnel. If necessary, raise the baby food jar by putting layers of clay under it.

**2.** Place the jar in the center of the baking tray. Pour the hydrogen peroxide into the jar. Moving quickly, stir in the yeast and set the funnel upside down over the jar. What happens?

## ACTION, REACTION, RESULTS

The combination of hydrogen peroxide and yeast produces a chemical reaction. The result is steam, foam, heat, and a hissing noise.

**A volcano is an opening in the Earth's crust. Under certain conditions, a volcano may erupt. When it does, lava, or molten rock, gases, ash, and large rocks are noisily forced out to the surface.**